Yachting 101

A Guide to the Basics of Buying, Renting and Sailing Yachts

By Jeffrey Pewitt

circumstances is the author responsible for any losses, direct or indirect, which are incurred as a result of the use of information contained within this document, including, but not limited to, —errors, omissions, or inaccuracies.

Contents

Thank you for buying this book and I hope that you will find it useful. If you will want to share your thoughts on this book, you can do so by leaving a review on the Amazon page, it helps me out a lot.

Introduction

Owning a yacht is by no means a little financial endeavor. Yachts can vary in price from a couple of thousand dollars to essentially limitless. It's not uncommon to see them auctioning for more than a couple of million dollars. Even if you choose a less costly yacht, you need to think about upkeep.

Every year you can anticipate spending about 10% of the overall price of your yacht in upkeep. A Yacht is a kind of boat; as such, it will remain in the water for the majority of its life. Continuous contact with the elements and with water takes its toll. This is magnified ten-fold if you have your yacht on seawater. Salt and other minerals wreak outright havoc on the exterior of the yacht along with the mechanical parts inside.

Aside from initial expense and upkeep, you get to stress over licenses and allows you to utilize your yacht depending upon where you live. If your yacht is bound for sea, you'll most likely wish to have a port to keep it at. The majority of these locations will have a month-to-month rate of around $15/ft. and generally, have a minimum (such as 30 ft. minimum). For an average-sized yacht of 45ft, you're looking at $675 a month, just for your yacht to have a place to remain!

Before you choose if owning a yacht is truly for you, make certain you think about the financial and logistical difficulties that lay ahead. Owning a yacht is a very enjoyable and satisfying experience that you'll delight in for many years to come. All the same, if you're not financially or psychologically ready to own and preserve a yacht, it could be a choice you wind up regretting a long time down the road. If you're sure that you are totally prepared to get in the world of yacht ownership, or at least yacht enthusiasm, then let's get going! We'll begin at the bare-bones fundamentals, and before you know it, you'll be a genuine professional on what a yacht is, how you can purchase or rent one and where you ought to take it as soon as you get it!

Chapter 1: What is a Yacht?

A yacht is a leisure boat, frequently of a high-end variety. The term originated from the Dutch Jacht, meaning "hunt." It was initially specified as a light, quick sailing vessel utilized by the Dutch navy to pursue pirates and other criminals around and into the shallow waters of the Low Nations. After its selection by Charles II of England as the vessel of choice to go back to Britain from Holland for his repair, it became utilized to convey important people.

In contemporary use, the term designates 2 rather various classes of watercraft, sailing and powerboats. Yachts are separate from working ships primarily by their leisure purpose, and it was not up until the increase of the steamboat and other kinds of powerboat that cruising vessels, in general, became viewed as high-end, or recreational vessels. Later on, the term came to include motorboats for mostly private satisfaction purposes too.

Yacht lengths normally vary from 20 feet up to hundreds of feet. A high-end craft that is tinier than 40 feet is more typically called a cabin cruiser or just a "cruiser." A mega yacht typically refers to any yacht (sail or power) above 100 ft. and a superyacht usually refers to any yacht over 200 ft. This size is little in relation to common cruise liners and oil tankers.

Chapter 2: History

Yacht (pronounced like "Yott" where it rhymes with "pot") was initially defined as a light, quick sailing vessel utilized by the Dutch navy to pursue pirates and other criminals around and into the shallow waters of the Low Countries. They were additionally utilized for non-military governmental functions such as customs responsibilities and delivering pilots to waiting ships. The latter use drew in the attention of rich Dutch merchants who started to develop private yachts so they could be taken out to welcome their returning ships.

Soon rich people started to utilize their 'Jachts' for pleasure trips. By the start of the 17th century, 'Jachts' came in 2 broad classifications- speel-jachts for sport and oorlog-jachts for naval tasks. By the middle of the century, big 'jacht' fleets were discovered around the Dutch coast and the Dutch states organized big 'evaluations' of private and war yachts for special events, therefore putting in place the foundation for the modern-day sport of yachting. Jachts of this period differed considerably in size, from around 40 ft. in length to being equal to the lower classes of the ship of the line. All had a type of fore/aft gaff rig with a flat bottom and lee boards to enable operations in shallow waters. The gaff rig remained the primary rig discovered on little European yachts for centuries up until giving way to the 'Bermudan sloop' rig in the 1960s.

Charles II of England spent part of his time in exile throughout the duration of the Commonwealth of England in the Netherlands and ended up being keen on sailing. He went back to England in 1660 aboard a Dutch yacht. Throughout his reign, Charles commissioned 24 Royal Yachts on top of the two provided to him by Dutch states on his remediation. As the fashion for yachting spread across the English upper class, yacht races started to end up being common. Other abundant people in Europe constructed yachts as the sport spread. Yachting, for that reason, ended up being a purely leisure form of sailing without any business or military function, which still serves a broad definition of both the sport and of the vessel.

Chapter 3: How Are Yachts Made?

Up until the 1950s, almost all yachts were made from wood or steel, however, a much broader range of materials is utilized today. Although wood hulls are still in production, the most typical construction material is fiberglass, followed by aluminum, steel, carbon fiber, and ferro-cement (rarer due to insurance troubles). Making use of wood has actually changed and is no longer confined to standard board-based techniques, however, it also consists of contemporary items like plywood, veneers and epoxy resins. Wood is primarily utilized by enthusiasts or wooden boat perfectionists when constructing a private boat.

Categories of Yachts

Sailing Yachts

Sailing yachts can vary in overall length (Length Over All-- LOA, in yachting parlance) from about 20 ft. to more than 100 ft., where the difference between a yacht and a ship ends up being blurred. Many independently owned yachts fall in the range of about 25-- 45 ft.; the expense of building and keeping a yacht increases rapidly as length boosts. In the U.S., sailors tend to refer to tinier yachts as sailboats, while referring to the basic sport of sailing as yachting. Within the restricted context of sailboat racing, a yacht is any sailing vessel participating in a race, despite the size.

Modern yachts have effective sail-plans, most significantly the Bermuda rig, that enables them to sail towards the wind. This ability is the outcome of a sail-plan and hull design.

Day Sailing Yachts

Day sailing yachts are generally little, at less than 20 ft. in length. Often called dinghies, they typically have a retractable keel, centerboard, or daggerboard. The majority of day-sailing yachts do not have a cabin, as they are developed for hourly or day-to-day usage and not for overnight journeys. At best, they might have a 'cubby,' where the front part of the hull has a raised strong roof to offer a location to store tools or to provide a standard shelter from wind or spray.

Weekender Yachts

Weekender yachts are a little bigger, at less than 30 ft. in length. They frequently have twin keels or raising keels, such as in trailer sailors. This enables them to run in shallow waters, and if required, "dry out"-- end up being beached as the tide falls. The hull shape (or twin-keel layout) enables the boat to sit upright when there is no water. Such boats are developed to undertake brief journeys, seldom lasting more than 2 or 3 days.

In coastal locations, long trips might be carried out in a series of brief hops. Weekenders generally have just a simple cabin, typically consisting of a single "saloon" with beds for two to three individuals. Smart use of ergonomics enables area in the saloon for a galley (kitchen area), seating, and navigation tools. There is a limited area for stores of water and food.

Many are single-misted "Bermuda sloops" (not to be puzzled with the kind of conventional Bermudian ship called a Bermuda sloop), with a single foresail of the jib or genoa type and a single mainsail (one variation of the previously mentioned Bermuda rig). Some are gaff rigged. The tiniest of this type, usually called pocket yachts or pocket cruisers, and trailer sailors can be transferred on unique trailers.

Cruising Yachts

Cruising yachts are by far the most frequent yachts in private usage, comprising the majority of the 25 to 45 ft. range. These vessels can be rather intricate in design, as they require a balance in between docile handling qualities, interior space, great light-wind functionality and on-board convenience. The big range of such craft, from lots of builders worldwide, makes it difficult to provide a single illustrative description. Nevertheless, many favor a teardrop-planform hull, with a large, flat bottom and deep single-fin keel to offer great stability. The majority of are single-masted Bermuda rigged sloops, with a single fore-sail of the jib or Genoa type and a single mainsail.

Spinnaker sails, in numerous sizes, are typically provided for down-wind usage. These types are frequently selected as family vessels, specifically those in the 26 to 40-foot variety. Such a vessel will typically have lots of cabins beneath the deck. Normally there will be 3 double-berth cabins, a single big saloon with galley, seating and navigation tools, and a "head" consisting of a toilet and shower room.

A lot of big yachts, 50 ft. and up, are additionally cruisers, however, their designs differ considerably as they are frequently "one-off" designs customized to the particular requirements of the purchaser. The interior is frequently finished in wood paneling, with a lot of storage space. Cruisers are rather capable of handling long-range passages of thousands of miles. Such boats have a cruising speed upwards of 6 knots. This fundamental design is common in the basic types produced by significant yacht-builders.

High-end Sailing Yachts

High-end Sailing Yachts are usually 82 ft. or longer. Just recently these kinds of yachts have actually adjusted and evolved from basic sailing boats to advanced, glamorous ships. This is mainly due to decreased hull-building expenses thanks to the introduction of fiberglass hulls and increased automation and assembly line methods for yacht building, particularly in Europe.

Every contemporary convenience from TV and Electrical Power to Restrooms and, sometimes, even tennis courts can be discovered on very large high-end yachts (130ft and bigger). These are typically really automated and utilize things like computer-controlled winches to adjust the sails. This needs extremely specialized and devoted power generation systems. Electrical power usage in yachts has actually come a long way in the past couple of years.

Even in the early 90's, it was not common for a 25-foot yacht to have electrical lighting. Now all but the tiniest, a lot of standard yachts have electrical lighting, radio, and navigation aids like Global Positioning Systems. Yachts around 33 ft. typically have amenities such as hot water, pressurized water supply, and fridges along with radar, echo-sounding and autopilot systems. In this case, the auxiliary engine additionally carries out the crucial function of powering a generator to supply electrical power and to recharge the yacht's batteries. For yachts engaged on long-range cruising, wind-, water- and solar-powered generators can carry out the identical function.

Racing Yachts

Racing yachts attempt to minimize the wetted surface area, which produces drag, by keeping the hull light whilst having a deep and heavy bulb keel, enabling them to support a high mast with an excellent sail area. Modern designs tend to have an extremely broad beam and a flat bottom, to offer buoyancy, preventing an extreme heel angle. Speeds of approximately 35 knots can be achieved in severe conditions.

Devoted offshore racing yachts compromise crew convenience for speed, having standard accommodation to decrease weight. Depending upon the kind of race, such a yacht might have a crew of 15 or more. Big inshore racing yachts might have a crew of 30. At the other extreme are "single-handed" races, where a single person alone needs to manage the yacht.

Yacht races might be over a basic course of just a couple of miles, as in the harbor racing of the International One Design; long-distance, open-ocean races, such as the Bermuda Race; or legendary trans-global contests like the Global Challenge, Volvo Ocean Race, and Clipper Round the World Race.

Propulsion

The motive force being the wind, sailing is more cost-effective and eco-friendly than any other means of propulsion. A hybrid kind of vessel is a motor sailing yacht that can utilize either voyage or propulsion (or both) as conditions determine.

Numerous "pure" sailing yachts are likewise geared up with a low-power internal-combustion engine for usage in conditions of calm and when going into or leaving hard anchorages. Vessels less than 25 ft. in length usually carry a petrol outboard-motor of between 5 and 40 horsepower (3.5 and 30 kW). Bigger vessels have in-board diesel engines of between 20 and 100 horsepower (15 and 75 kW) depending upon size. In the usual 25 to 45-foot class, engines of 20 to 40 horsepower are the most frequent.

Hull Types

Monohull yachts are usually fitted with a fixed keel or a centerboard (adjustable keel) beneath the waterline to counterbalance the overturning force of the wind on the vessel's sails. Multihull yachts utilize 2 hulls (catamarans) or 3 (trimarans) extensively separated from each other to offer a steady base that withstands overturning and enables sailing in shallower waters.

Motor Yachts

Motor yachts normally suit the following categories:

- Day cruiser yacht (no cabin, sporadic amenities like fridge and plumbing).

- Weekender yacht (a couple of standard cabins, standard galley appliances and plumbing).

- Cruising yacht (adequate amenities to enable living aboard for extended durations).

- Sport fishing yacht (yacht with living amenities and sporting fishing tools).

- High-end yacht (comparable to the last 3 kinds of yachts, with more elegant finishings/amenities).

Propulsion.

Motor yachts generally have a couple of internal combustion engines that burn diesel fuel. Biodiesel for marine propulsion remains in the experimental phase (e.g. Earthrace). Depending upon engine size, fuel expenses might make motor yachts more pricey to run than sailing yachts. Nevertheless, for tinier engine sizes, operating expenses are comparable to sailing vessels, because of the high expense of sails, which need regular replacement.

Hull types.

The shape of a motor yacht's hull might be based upon displacement, planing, or in between. Although monohulls have actually long been the standard in motor yachts, multihulls are gaining in appeal.

Chapter 4: How to Purchase a Yacht.

This is a sensitive topic since yachts can vary in price from a couple of thousand dollars to numerous millions of dollars! Depending upon what sort of yacht you're trying to find and simply how luxurious you want to get, it might be eventually more inexpensive just to rent a yacht. Before you buy a yacht, keep in mind the very first part of this book. Do you have the funds to buy the yacht? Can you afford about 10% of that every year for upkeep? Do you have a place to put your yacht or a way to pay for porting? If you answered yes to all of those questions then you're prepared to begin searching for a yacht.

The Basic Idea

- Secure your finances. You must comprehend how you will fund the boat before you ever step foot in a yacht display room. Without correct funding, a boat has a really excellent odds of ending up being a hole in the water into which you'll wind up pouring cash. Likewise, comprehending your financing will provide a strong idea of your budget plan.

- Choose between brand-new and pre-owned yachts. Both the brand-new and pre-owned yacht markets are big and active, and both have advantages and drawbacks. New boats are sold at an extremely high premium when compared to fairly brand-new used boats. Pre-owned yachts, nevertheless, might be more affordable, but consist of a specific amount of danger and unpredictability about the boat's history and structural integrity.

- Know your purposes for the yacht. A harbor gem developed to show your buddies and have lunch on is an extremely different boat than a significant cruiser or ocean-going vessel. You want to understand precisely what you'll be utilizing the yacht for before you purchase anything.

- Think about a brokerage. If you're looking to the upper end of the marketplace, a brokerage can offer you a bit of guarantee that the boat originated from a respectable owner and remains in good condition. If you do not wish to spend excessive cash, take a look at your local marinas to see what's out there.

- Get a professional survey. Having a professional survey the boat is not an option. You should get the boat completely checked for any damage or issues before you even seriously think about buying it. Work with an expert to complete this vital part of the procedure

Advanced Tips

Used or New?

Consider your choice of brand-new or used thoroughly. There is a lot of value in used boats. More first time purchasers buy brand-new boats, while skilled boaters more frequently purchase used. And with excellent reason. Experienced boaters understand that there is a better value dollar for dollar in lots of used boats than brand-new ones. They have actually already had the experience of taking a big hit in devaluation, together with the high expense of funding associated with a brand-new boat purchase. To help choose which is right for you, think about the following.

When we track the devaluation curve for a number of the most popular builder's designs by figuring out the net yearly loss in resale worth, we discover that the greater the vessel quality, the quicker the devaluation curve will flatten out. That indicates that higher-quality boats proportionately lose less value than lower-quality vessels. For those builders, the flattening out generally begins around 5 years, so that by the time a vessel is 6 years of age, the yearly loss of value is just a few percentage points.

If you really wish to know what the yearly expense of ownership is, add in the overall principal and interest to the yearly operation and upkeep expenses. Then, just deduct the expected residual valve and divide it by the number of years owned. For a brand-new boat, this can be a massive sum each and every year. Carry out the identical calculation for the purchase of an 8-year-old vessel and the expense of ownership comes to just a fraction of that of a brand-new vessel.

A basic guideline is that a brand-new boat purchase works out much better for the owner who keeps a boat longer than the average 4 years, or at least through the bottoming out of the devaluation curve. Clearly, the longer a boat is owned, the less the yearly expense ends up being. Nevertheless, that does not help much as far as residual value is concerned unless we think about the initial expense versus expected resale value.

As soon as we do this, we comprehend that what they told us was actually correct: boats, like cars, are not an investment but a significant expenditure. If you plan just to own the vessel for a couple of years, or you expect that there is a possibility you might need to sell, without a doubt, a used boat will be a better choice.

Gasoline & Diesel Engines

Within the size range of 25-35 feet, it is a misconception that diesel power is more affordable than gas. After about 4 years, diesel engines end up being a lot more pricey to own and take care of. When a gas engine goes bad, it can be restored or changed for a couple of thousand dollars while we measure the expenses of diesel overhauls in the tens of thousands. Unless one intends to get a great deal of usage from his boat, gas engines are typically a better option for boats up to 35 feet.

With used boats, do not make the mistake of equating low hour meter readings with excellent engine condition. Generally, engine hours mean little since engines degrade in time. Engines that are little used, gas or diesel, are often in worse condition for the absence of use. Additionally, do not succumb to the misconception that marine diesels last for countless hours. They do not. The average time between significant repairs is around 6-7 years. Marine engines degrade quickly in a saltwater environment.

Excellent boats with bad engines can end up being a bargain when comparing price differentials against a more recent boat purchase, especially for tinier boats, and boats with gas engines where engine replacements are easier. Lots of purchasers discover that they can get a bargain in a boat with clapped out engines and restoring or replacing them. If you do not mind the hassle, it might be worth making the price contrast. If the price works out, you wind up with a boat with brand-new engines, a genuine comfort to any boat owner.

While used boats can represent good value, this holds true just up to a point. The issue with some boats, when they get beyond 10-12 years, is postponed upkeep. It is a regrettable fact of life that numerous boat owners cut a great deal of corners when making repairs, additions or enhancements.

This is especially true when it pertains to mechanical, electrical and plumbing. While the interior might be stunning, significant systems might have been overlooked. On good quality boats, repairs are frequently done to a much lower standard than initially, so that by the time a decade has actually passed, there might be a great deal of subpar maintenance and jury-rigging.

Likewise, keep in mind what kind of boat you're purchasing. Some boats have hull parts that are totally closed off and can not be accessed. These do not present issues for brand-new boat owners; however, after years of wear and tear, there might be leakages in those locations. Considering that the hulls are sealed off, you have no chance of understanding or having the ability to patch the leakages in an emergency.

In addition to buying price, interest and devaluation, the expense of ownership consists of repair and maintenance, something owners seldom think about. For brand-new boats, upkeep is low for the first 3 years or two. After 3 years, expenses begin increasing considerably. No matter the type, significant machinery will typically need significant repairs in years 5-7. There's a reason why warranties expire when they do, and that's since that's when the breakdowns start to take place. If you purchase a brand-new 40' motor yacht and sell it after 3-4 years, yearly upkeep is most likely to average around 4%. The longer you own it, the more it is going to increase as things wear out and break down. The very first big hit normally comes when an engine or generator goes bad anywhere between 5-7 years. Undoubtedly, if you own the vessel this long, all of a sudden, the yearly average takes a huge leap. If you're purchasing used, then you need to be prepared for this, whether it's an unanticipated blister repair job, or some other issue that's not covered by insurance. Obviously, with a used boat, that fifty or a hundred thousand you saved off the brand-new price more than offsets "huge expense."

The point is that in putting together averages, with time, we understand that expenses can be decreased to yearly percentages for which an owner must be prepared. For twin screw diesel motor yachts or fishermen, a ten-year average will run around 7% yearly. This represents all kinds of upkeep from bottom painting to pump replacements and engine overhauls. Additionally, this presumes that there is little or no deferred upkeep. If you're entering into a used boat with substantial deferred upkeep, that yearly average can increase drastically, specifically when major issues gang up on you simultaneously.

Purchase Agreements

Ensure that your purchase contract enables you to cancel the deal if the vessel does not satisfy your requirements. Include a stipulation that the sea trial needs to be carried out in open water for a minimum of 2 hours.

If the seller warrants that he will fix any flaws, make certain that you get that in writing, ideally with a maximum dollar quantity attached. It is not smart to enable the seller to fix shortages himself. The reason ought to be apparent, however, lots of purchasers ignore the possibility that the repairs that the seller makes might not be acceptable. Certainly, they frequently aren't. The very best procedure is to negotiate a dollar decrease to the sales price and make the repairs yourself, even if there is an aspect of unpredictability regarding cost. Naturally, you ought to get expense estimates on deficiencies, and better still, an agreement price.

If you can't get away from the seller making repairs, at least specify in the agreement that the repair company needs to be mutually agreeable to both purchaser and seller. What you're aiming to avoid is the shade-tree mechanic who does not get the job done right.

Keep in mind that the broker represents the seller, not you, the purchaser. If you wish to believe their representations, make them put it in writing. That way, you have an agreement, not only a sales pitch.

When concluding the deal, do not be too fast to condemn an otherwise great boat that has a significant issue, such as a bad engine. If you have actually done your research and have actually looked into more than simply a couple of boats, you understand what is available and at what cost. The old saying that the devil you know is much better than the one you do not applies.

If you can get serious flaws fixed well within the financial range, you'll most likely wind up with a better boat than the next one you look at. The reason is easy: if the issue has actually manifested, it has actually ended up being understood. When you're taking a look at boats of similar age, odds are those boats are likewise well en route to having comparable issues. For that reason, the more issues that can be found and fixed, the better off you'll be.

To Review

- Make quality a significant factor to consider. Do not attempt to get the biggest vessel that your budget plan will enable. Better to take a step down in size and a step up in quality.

- If the size is a significant factor to consider, seriously think about used versus brand-new as a means of remaining within your budget.

- Look beyond attractive interiors, elegant upholstery and fancy designs: the charm might just be skin deep.

- Calculate the complete expense of ownership, including devaluation, interest, insurance, dockage, fuel and repairs. Figure upkeep as a yearly percentage over the duration of ownership.

- Seriously think about gas instead of diesel for boats under 35' for which you do not expect to get much usage.

- As soon as you have actually selected numerous possibilities, take a tour of a marina or boatyard and see how the products of those builders hold up throughout the years. Speak with their owners and see what they have to say.

- Consult a surveyor before you make the purchase. The majority of surveyors will be glad to help you choose.

- Take the time to discover the very best surveyor in your location.

- Make your purchase decision just after you have actually read the survey report

- Think about the benefit of getting significant machinery or parts revamped or replaced based upon a decrease in price.

Chapter 5: How to Lease a Yacht

Individuals who do not have the time or financial access to buy their own yacht can still take pleasure in the trip and high-end of a yacht holiday or weekend. Owning a yacht is a huge dedication of time, which the majority of people do not have. Anybody who wishes to take a weekend trip or perhaps a longer yachting getaway can do so by renting a yacht. This is an affordable and time-saving alternative to owning one. If your plans just include a periodic trip, renting a yacht might be a smarter alternative too. If you wish to cruise the open seas, yet you do not wish to buy your own yacht, simply rent one for a week or two. Yachts are an excellent way to experience the sea while still having all the conveniences of the house.

Here are the steps you can take to start with your Yacht:

1. Choose where you're going on your trip. This will help identify which company the yacht is going to need to be rented from. Although there are lots of companies out there that provide yacht rentals, they might not be found at your planned location. Some yacht rental companies even restrict the destinations of their yachts. If there are a restricted number of rentals available from your preferred company at the time of the holiday, think about altering the destination or travel time, because the appropriate rental company can make all of the difference.

2. Call the rental company in the area of departure to discover pricing information, any limitations they put on the rental of yachts and the insurance requirements. Request all of the specs that will add expenses and limit the yachting experience. Numerous companies will have sites with all of their information. Or, you can have a travel agent find the business and call them for you; a travel agent or yacht broker can help plan the holiday and protect all the information.

3. Make a list of the amenities that the yacht must have to make the journey enjoyable. Plan a budget plan of just how much can be spent on these amenities. Note the amenities in order of priority. Not all yachts will have all the amenities, so be ready to understand which ones are optional and which ones are needed. This list is going to help narrow the yacht options.

4. Travel to a neighborhood boat show to discover high-end yachts owned by private people who have an interest in renting them. These high-end yachts can rent for an elegant amount of cash; however, if the travel group is big, it might be worth the additional cost. Going to a boat program will additionally supply a chance to explore the various kinds of yachts prior to deciding which rental to pick.

5. Keep in mind the fundamentals. Discover in advance if the rental charges consist of fuel expenses, food and beverage expenditures, customs fees, taxes or any other expenses. Get information on what, if any, staff will accompany you on the yacht and which services they'll offer.

6. Get a written contract about the overall expenses of the yacht rental. Learn just how much the rental charge, in fact, is and if this consists of fuel expenses. Make sure to think about the expenses of food and beverages, any custom-made charges that might be incurred when taking a trip, taxes that might need to be paid, and so on. Will the rental fee consist of a captain or a staff, and if so, how many staff members are going to be on board and what will each one supervise? Discovering all the costs and associated details will make the yacht rental trip satisfying and relaxing.

How To Get A Free Yacht!

Okay, so the title of this part appears a little sensationalist. Certainly, this is not going to work 100% of the time; however, the point of this book is to entice individuals of all budget plans so if purchasing and renting standard yachts is way out of your price range, this might be the answer for you!

Wooden Boat magazine has a "free boats" part in every issue.

Any harbormaster can demonstrate to you some free boats.

They're specifically numerous in the northeast in the fall.

Divorce season, whenever that is, produces great deals of project boats that

 "should be eliminated from my yard prior to such-and-such a date."

Chapter 6: Yacht and Boat Protection Tips!

Personal Yacht Safety

Have you just recently made plans to charter a private yacht? If so, when is your journey coming? Is it rapidly approaching? While the chartering of a private yacht can be enjoyable and amazing, it is additionally essential that you put a focus on protection. When on a privately chartered yacht, you are actually at the mercy of the waters and your yacht team. Although it might look like the circumstance is out of your hands, there are a variety of various manners in which you can set about securing yourself. Simply a few of those ways are discussed below.

Maybe, the very best thing that you can do is tour your yacht. Although you may wish to begin enjoying your getaway immediately, you will additionally wish to know the ins and outs of your yacht. Whether you decide to explore every inch of the yacht yourself or if you ask the team to provide you a fast tour, you are encouraged to do so. In case of an emergency, this might come in helpful.

In addition to getting a generalized tour of your privately chartered yacht, you are going to additionally wish to know about safety, specifically where the safety tools or supplies are. All privately chartered yachts must come geared up with things like lifejackets or floatable rafts. While these things might assist you in an emergency situation, you need to understand where they are initially. It might additionally be a great idea to find out how to send a call for help in case anything occurs to your yacht crew. It is additionally essential to understand where all first aid items, like first aid kits, are.

Similar to any trip that you take, you are encouraged to understand where you are going and when. This information must not just be utilized on your own, but it needs to be provided to your friends and family additionally. For example, does your privately chartered yacht adventure include docking in foreign ports? If so, you will certainly wish to let your buddies or members of the family understand where you will be going. If you are not provided a copy of your travel plan, you are urged to produce your own. Give a couple of copies of that travel plan to those that you know. Should you not return when you are expected to, they might have the ability to call the appropriate authorities.

Considering that you will, basically, be vacationing on the open waters, it is recommended that you understand how to swim. Although lots of privately chartered yacht journeys go off without a hitch, you never ever actually know. That is why it is encouraged that you understand how to swim. If you do not consider yourself to be a skilled swimmer, you might wish to consider taking a refresher training course. If you are taking a trip with children, it is additionally recommended that they understand how to swim. Lots of local community centers, like YMCA's, provide inexpensive or economically priced swimming lessons, for people of all ages. For your own security and even a sense of security, you are encouraged to take one of these training courses or lessons.

While the above-mentioned security suggestions might be able to help you remain safe, it is additionally crucial to keep in mind that there are some scenarios that might be out of your hands. Because of that, you are advised to check out travel insurance, specifically if you are intending on chartering a private yacht for a prolonged time period.

General Boating Security Suggestions

Be Weather-Wise

Constantly check local weather conditions for boating safety the day before and of departure. TV and radio forecasts could be a great source of information. If you discover darkening clouds, rough changing winds, or unexpected drops in temperature level, play it safe by getting off the water. View the existing forecast by postal code.

Follow A Pre-Departure Checklist

Correct boating security implies being prepared for any possibility on the water. From security guideline compliance to suggestions on refueling, following a pre-departure list is the most effective way to ensure no boating safety guidelines or preventative measures have actually been forgotten. Things to include in your checklist:

o Have I inspected the weather condition?

o Are my boat license and registration current?

o Have I made myself acquainted with the area I am going to?

o Check the tide to make sure the ramp is appropriate for launching.

o Checked the boat for problems and noted any needed repairs.

o Do I have ample fuel for the round trip, plus reserves?

o Do I have ample water and food for the return trip, plus reserves?

o Are all the suitable safety tools on board and in working order?

o Have I demonstrated to my passengers where the security tools are and how to utilize them?

o Have I advised a trusted individual of my boating plan? This is ideally jotted down and handed to the individual prior to your departure. Feature where you are going and when you intend to be back along with the number of passengers on board and the kind of radio and emergency beacon you are bringing. These details are really valuable in an emergency situation.

A few of the following safety tools are required by law - you must examine the laws with your local authority. Security tools can include:

o Oars

o Knife

o Rope

o Radio

o Torch

o Mirror

o Flares

o Boat hook

o First aid kit

o Drinking water

o Fire extinguisher

o Bailer or bucket

o Chart and compass

o Anchor chain and rope

o Buoyancy aids, life vest

o Emergency Position Indicating Radio Beacon (EPIRB).

Utilize Common Sense.

Among the most vital parts of boating security is to utilize your common sense. This indicates operating at a safe speed at all times, particularly in hectic areas. Be alert at all times. Stay away from big vessels and boats that can be restricted in their capability to stop or turn. Additionally, be considerate of buoys and other navigational aids, all of which have actually been positioned there for one reason just- to guarantee your own boating security.

Designate an Assistant Skipper.

Ensure more than a single person on board is familiar with all elements of your boat's handling and safe operation. If the main navigator is hurt or immobilized in any way, it is necessary to ensure another person can follow the appropriate boating security guidelines to get everybody else back to coast.

Establish A Float Strategy.

Whether you choose to notify a member of the family or staff at your neighborhood marina, constantly make sure to let somebody else understand your float plan in regards to where you're going and for how long you're going to be gone.

A float plan can consist of the following information: name, address, and telephone number of trip leader: name and number of all travelers; boat type and registration information; trip travel plan; kinds of communication and signal tools onboard.

Make Appropriate Use Of Lifejackets.

Did you understand that most drowning victims as the outcome of boating mishaps were discovered not to be using a lifejacket? Numerous individuals all over the world lose their lives each year in leisure boating mishaps and the majority of them are from drowning. Make certain that your friends and family aren't part of this figure by appointing and fitting each member of your onboard team with a lifejacket prior to departure. See link beneath to learn more on lifejackets.

The Facts About Boating And Alcohol

One third of all boating deaths involve alcohol. The blood alcohol limitation on the water is the same as on the roads--0.05%. Additional care is required as the wind; waves and the sun merge to increase the impact of alcohol. Your opportunities for disorientation and drowning are significantly increased.

Learn to Swim

If you're going to remain in and around the water, appropriate boating security implies understanding how to swim.

Take A Boating Course

Starting boaters and knowledgeable professionals alike need to be familiar with boating security guidelines of operation. Boater education requirements differ by state- some need validated completion of at least one boating security course. Despite your individual state's requirements, it's constantly essential to be educated, informed and prepared for every scenario that may occur. It might save your life or the life of somebody you love.

You can discover boating security guidelines by taking a local community course.

Kid's Safety

Purchase an excellent lifejacket or life vest with a collar that turns a kid face-up in the water. It needs to have a strong waist and crotch straps, a handle on the collar, and ideally be a bright yellow or orange color for great visibility.

Connect a plastic security whistle to the Lifejacket and teach the kid how to utilize the whistle - and practice utilizing it. In addition, guarantee that kids completely comprehend security procedures and can react properly in an emergency situation. Practice security drills and scenario role-plays so that emergency procedures end up being second nature to you and your kids.

Check out the Yacht & Boat Directory for Kid's Lifejackets.

NSW Maritime urges it is a must to have a lifejacket readily available for all individuals on board, and it needs to remain in good condition, ready at hand, and of the appropriate size. Lifejackets are available in a wide variety of sizes to fit grownups down to kids. For infants where a correctly-sized lifejacket is not obtainable, NSW Maritime advises parents to keep the kid close at all times while afloat and to have their own lifejacket prepared for instantaneous usage or to put it on at times of increased danger. Increased danger consists of instances when conditions get rough, like when a storm approaches.

While it is just mandatory to use a lifejacket in NSW while crossing coastal bars, riding a jet ski or in a paddle craft or windsurfer more than 400m from shore, Maritime advises that kids and bad swimmers wear it at all times when in the open spots of a boat which is underway.

Kids should additionally be kept within the bounds of the vessel and must never ever sit with their legs or arms dangling over the edges of a powerboat that is underway.

The activity called 'teak surfing' where individuals, generally kids, hang onto the duckboard or transom of a powerboat that is underway is

 unsafe and must not be promoted. Not just is a kid near to the prop in such a scenario, they are additionally likely to be exposed to carbon monoxide poisoning by means of exhaust fumes.

Bring A Marine Radio

A cellphone is insufficient. It can just reach a single person, and can end up being water damaged really quickly; run out of battery or the reception can drop out. If something fails with your mobile, your lifeline to safety is gone. A 'Mayday' call-out on a Marine Radio can be heard by many individuals - immediately, getting assistance to you faster. It is additionally purpose-built and is a lot more dependable than a cellphone.

Night Safety

When night falls, it is a totally different world on the water, therefore, vessels that run from sunset to sunrise, whether at anchor or underway, should bring and display the appropriate lights.

Chapter 7: Popular Yachting Events

America's Cup

The America's Cup is a trophy granted to the winner of the America's Cup sailing regatta match, and the earliest active trophy in global sport.

Initially called the Royal Yacht Squadron Cup, it ended up being referred to as the "America's Cup" after the first yacht to win the trophy, the schooner America. The trophy stayed in the hands of the New York Yacht Club (NYYC) from 1857 (when the syndicate that won the Cup donated the trophy to the club) up until 1983 when the Cup was won by the Royal Perth Yacht Club, with their yacht, Australia II, concluding the longest winning streak in the history of sport.

The America's Cup regatta is a challenge-driven series of match races between 2 yachts, which is regulated by the Deed of Gift, which is the legal file that made the cup available for worldwide competition. Any yacht club that fulfills the requirements defined in the Deed of Gift can challenge the yacht club that holds the Cup. If the challenging yacht club wins the match, the stewardship of the cup is passed on to that yacht club.

From the 3rd defense of the Cup in 1876 through the twentieth defense in 1967, there was constantly one challenger and one protector, although the NYYC ran a protector choice series to choose the yacht they would utilize in the match. Beginning in 1970, interest in challenging was so strong that the NYYC began enabling several challengers to run a selection regatta amongst themselves with the winner being replaced as Challenger and going on to the actual America's Cup match. From 1983 up until 2007, Louis Vuitton sponsored the Louis Vuitton Cup as a prize for the winner of the challenger choice series.

The Cup draws in leading sailors and yacht designers due to its long history and status. It is not just a test of sailing ability, boat and sail design, yet additionally of fund-raising and management abilities. From the initial defense in 1870, the matches were between large (65 ft. or greater on the waterline) racing yachts owned by rich sportspeople. This culminated in races in spectacular J-class yachts in 1930, 1934 and 1937.

After the second world war, nearly twenty years passed without a difficulty, so the New York Yacht Club made changes to the Deed to enable the tinier and less costly 12-meter class yachts to contend, and this class was utilized up until 1987 when it was switched out by the International America's Cup Class.

Places to Take Your Yacht

The Mediterranean

This is most likely the ideal location on the planet to see yachts and be seen on them. From the French Riviera to the Greek Isles, this body of water is loaded with every manner of pleasure craft throughout the European summer season. The principality of enjoyment, Monaco, is the informal capital of the global yachting community and stomping premises of royalty and the jet set. Nice and Cannes swell with a population as the temperature level increases and the Hollywood set makes the yearly trip for the movie festival and associated festivity. However, these are, without a doubt, not the only Mediterranean locations of interest for yachters. Here are some proper destinations that you might find less congested and more enticing than the Côte d'Azur.

Ibiza

Ibiza will most likely appeal most to the more youthful crowd which chooses to stick around technology and be a part of the club scene. Ibiza is the world's clubbing capital with huge clubs that house unruly nightlife and even foam parties. As a hub for electronic music, this island draws in a young set that dance till dawn night after night. If dancing isn't your cup of tea, the island's history and natural landscapes can keep you amused for days.

Dubrovnik

Croatia might not look like a location that would be terrific for taking your yacht, however, the Dalmatian coast is ending up being the brand-new place to go experience the delights of Mediterranean life. Compared to 1950's Italy, the laid back environment and ancient walled city produce a great port of call along the Adriatic.

The Caribbean

The Caribbean is a stunning location with droves of palms and amazing sunset. The only problem is with the people that come and go from island to island, interfering with the peace that makes these islands fantastic. Remarkably, there is a part of the Caribbean that exists apart from Little Switzerland and all of the "Duty-Free" mania that comes with the notable islands.

Martinique

What makes Martinique a terrific island is a reality that although it is a quite populated location, only a couple of cruise ships dock here and the everyday life remains quite relaxed. The island is a French Overseas Department, suggesting that the island is technically French home turf and even votes in the French Assembly. This allows the island to boast the best highways and paved roadways in the Caribbean. Martinique is a fantastic location to see rainforests and the excellent volcano, Mt. Mount Pelée, which ruined the old capital, St. Pierre. If you wish to experience the lavish nature of Hawaii and do not want to make the long plane journey, Martinique is a terrific option.

The Spanish Virgin Islands

Culebra and Vieques are 2 islands that comprise this little group off the coast of Puerto Rico. Now, Vieques might have remained in the news for Navy bomb testings a while back, however, the armed forces are gone now and tourism is slowly coming alive. Beaches on both islands verge on the surreal and stay mainly deserted. Have a look at the bioluminescent bays which are loaded with microscopic life that glows with motion.

These choices offer you a peek of different Mediterranean and Caribbean, however, what if you wish to totally desert the beaten path and blaze a course to your own hideaway. Here are some places that offer excellent scenery and ensure a special, memorable yachting expedition.

Labrador

The northernmost Canadian Maritimes do not bring in a great deal of tourists, however, it isn't for the absence of something to see. A yacht offers a tourist the utmost accessibility to the remote communities of the Labrador. Charming fishing towns and scores of wildlife make the rocky shoreline a wonderful location for summertime. Yes, I say summertime just due to the fact that even in the heat of July, expect to see icebergs wandering along and keeping the trip interesting. A terrific photo log of a cruise to the Labrador could be discovered here.

The Amazon

Sure, a jungle expedition is enjoyable, however, why not experience the exotic with the convenience of air conditioning and a private chef? Sail up the magnificent river as far as your yacht will enable and see monkeys and pink dolphins. Bring the kids along for the ride too. They'll act if they understand that the waters are swarmed with Piranhas.

The Galapagos

Darwin might have been the initial outsider to value these weird islands, however, contemporary tourists will not be working on any popular theories whilst going to the Galapagos. The huge draw here is the wildlife and volcanic activity. Make certain to see the tortoise and different marine lizards. The islands are ending up being a tourist draw, however, the greatest cruise ships that tour these waters have less than 500 attendees.

Eventually, you and your captain need to choose the most effective travel plan for you and your yacht. Some places aren't made for the contemporary megayacht, but can quickly manage tinier vessels. The choices are endless; deserted beaches are plentiful for those with the means to get to them. A yacht, whether owned or chartered, could be the secret to going to locations that have not been altered by the ravages of mass tourism. Wherever you choose to sail, keep in mind to experience the culture and way of life. This is going to make your memories sweeter and the time you spend there even more precious. Bon Voyage!!

Hawaii

You can see surfers perform their incredible stunts on the big waves from your berth at the dock. Together with the strikingly gorgeous landscape, you can delight in a few of the most popular beaches worldwide. A Hawaii yacht charter getaway is the holiday you have actually always daydreamed about.

You can go to numerous coves and inlets throughout your Hawaii yacht charter, where you can be totally alone or with a loved one. On Moloka, the 3,800-foot cliffs are the greatest on the planet, and the Pelekunu Valley opens into an unoccupied area. You can moor your yacht off among the many golden beaches and row to coast in the dinghy. A Hawaii yacht charter is going to additionally provide you the chance to enjoy magnificent diving experiences, and you can take pleasure in the excitement of sliding down 10-foot and greater waves, something you will not discover on other tropical yacht charters.

Hawaiian sailing holidays are quick, much quicker than in the Caribbean. This makes Hawaii yacht charters popular with those who have actually been sailing for many years. Prior to taking a bareboat charter, you do need to have some understanding of cruising the waters around Hawaii. To help you have a safe Hawaiian getaway with a bareboat yacht charter, you want to understand such things as not taking a night trip on the water when the winds lay and avoiding heading to windward when the trade winds are up.

There are no state taxes in Hawaii. This is among the benefits of booking a Hawaii yacht charter for the sailing trip of your dreams. The estimated expense is what you pay. You do not need to figure in any additional money for taxes for a Hawaiian sailing trip. The director of the charter business will find the ideal yacht to fit your requirements and provide you choices so that you can tailor your Hawaiian trip.

Hawaii yacht charters consist of special charters for sundown dinners, occasions, activities, and formal celebrations, like weddings. You can select a yacht that just holds 6 travelers or as much as 49. The bigger yacht is powered in addition to the crew to allow you to delight in a private resort as you cruise the Hawaiian islands. You can schedule your Hawaii yacht charter online without even leaving the convenience of your home.

Inexpensive Florida Trips

You can quickly charter a boat in the U.S. State of Florida for a truly enjoyable and interesting family getaway experience. A couple of things match the satisfaction of the Atlantic breeze or lovely gulf ocean in a yacht on the eastern coastline, searching for simply the appropriate location to dock for a bit of enjoyment or shopping.

That seems like a terrific way to spend a summertime holiday, right? You're not the only individual who believes so; numerous businesses in the Miami area offer high-end yacht charters. Discovering a location to dock your yacht might be tough; having the ability to charter one is extremely handy, specifically if you live far from Florida. You may wish to check out companies that provide high-end yacht sales, or sales of other kinds of water vessels. Miami yacht charter companies can supply you with information.

Companies with Yacht Chartering Services

Water Fantaseas, provides a range of cruise choices, serves the Ft. Lauderdale, Aventura, and Miami locations. Its services consist of corporate charters and lodgings for special occasions. They provide high-end sport yachts, high-end motor yachts, party yachts, powerboats, fishing boats, high-end mega yachts, high-end cruising vessels, and catamarans, among other water vessels. They have term-charters along with half- and full-day charters. An exceptional company, it provides the best in top quality sea trips for those who desire the most out of their holiday.

You can additionally go on the internet at www.biscaynelady.com to have a look at Biscayne Lady Yacht Charters. You will be, actually, in the lap of luxury when you reserve one of their holiday charters. Whether you have an interest in a business or social event, a wedding event celebration, a twosome, or a solitary affair, they have all it requires to outfit you in style. Amongst the amenities their elegant yachts provide are 3 grand decks, lodgings for up to 400 travelers, catamaran-designed twin hulls, cutting edge exterior and interior designs and far more.

Florida Yacht Charters and Sales serves Miami Beach, Key West, and the Bahamas. The people at this business offer charters and guidelines, along with sales and service. For those thinking about an extensive yachting experience, they even provide membership for boaters to sign up with a yacht-sharing program called SailTime Miami. Their complete line of vessels consists of yachts, sailboats, catamarans, trawlers, bare boats, and motor yachts. With this wide range of crafts to pick from, and amenities that will please even the most critical of sailors, consumers are sure to discover what they desire.

Carrousel Yacht Extraordinaire, based in Miami, accommodates the requirements of its consumers in grand style. Whether you wish to host a vacation celebration, anniversary, wedding, reunion, graduation, birthday celebration, business meal, or simply escape by yourself, this company is a terrific way to go. You can additionally travel the Florida shoreline from Palm Beach, Boca Raton, Ft. Lauderdale, Hollywood, Aventura, Miami, and Miami Beach in the elegant chartered yacht of the day.

You can discover the ideal chartering service for your requirements in practically any waterside location worldwide by just bringing up your preferred online search engine and doing an online search. Up until you have actually experienced the luxury of cruising around the ocean on a chartered yacht, you're missing out on the holiday of a lifetime. There's a vessel out there prepared and waiting on you, whether you wish to escape by yourself or with family, buddies, business partners, or former schoolmates. Lots of companies are available to do their finest to satisfy your requirements and the requirements of your ocean-going celebration.

Conclusion: Enjoy Your Yacht

I have actually offered you all the fundamental information for obtaining your yacht. You've been completely briefed on purchasing methods, renting procedures and even a couple of pointers on getting a yacht free of charge. All you need to do now is enjoy your trip time with your yacht. Whether it's a small family yacht or a million-dollar party yacht, it's a wonderful vessel that is going to offer you an experience you simply can't get on land.

The essential last piece of recommendation I can provide you is to print out the safety suggestions in this book so that you always have them when you need them. There's nothing that ruins the satisfaction of owning a yacht like ending up being the victim of a dreadful boating accident. Pick a safe yacht that you can quickly navigate in and make certain you're constantly able to interact with the coast guard or local authorities.

Keep in mind that I provided a couple of vacation spot possibilities; however, there are countless other locations you might take your yacht to. Even merely cruising at your local pier can be a great way to unwind after a tough day's work. Constantly keep your yacht well managed, take note of all safety suggestions and you are going to get a lifetime worth of satisfaction from your party or family cruising yacht!

I hope that you enjoyed reading through this book and that you have found it useful. If you want to share your thoughts on this book, you can do so by leaving a review on the Amazon page. Have a great rest of the day.

Made in the USA
Middletown, DE
23 November 2019

79294062R00038